WOLFGANG AMADEUS MOZART

REQUIEM

für SATB soli, Chor und Orchester
for SATB Soli, Choir and Orchestra

d-Moll / D minor
KV 626 / SmWV 105

Ergänzung von / Completed by
Franz Xaver Süßmayr

Herausgegeben von / Edited by
David I. Black

Klavierauszug / Vocal Score

ALLE RECHTE VORBEHALTEN · ALL RIGHTS RESERVED

EDITION PETERS
LEIPZIG · LONDON · NEW YORK

INHALT / CONTENTS

Vorwort / Preface . . . . III/VI

Introitus · Kyrie
   1. Requiem *(Soprano solo, Coro)* 2
   2. Kyrie *(Coro)* 7

Sequenz
   3. Dies irae *(Coro)* 13
   4. Tuba mirum *(Soli)* 20
   5. Rex tremendae *(Coro)* 24
   6. Recordare *(Soli)* 27
   7. Confutatis *(Coro)* 37
   8. Lacrimosa *(Coro)* 42

Offertorium
   9. Domine Jesu *(Soli, Coro)* 45
  10. Hostias *(Coro)* 54

Sanctus · Benedictus
  11. Sanctus *(Coro)* 61
  12. Benedictus *(Soli, Coro)* 64

Agnus Dei
  13. Agnus Dei *(Coro)* 73

Communio
  14. Lux aeterna *(Soprano solo, Coro)* 77

Aufführungsdauer / Duration: ca. 60 Min.

Partitur / Full Score EP 11035
Aufführungsmaterial leihweise und käuflich erhältlich
Orchestral material is available for hire and purchase

Vorwort

Das Requiem KV 626, Mozarts einzige Komposition einer *missa pro defunctis*, geht auf einen Auftrag des Grafen Franz von Wallsegg (1763–1827) zurück.[1] Wallseggs Gattin Anna, geborene Prenner von Flammberg, war am 14. Februar 1791 im Alter von 20 Jahren verstorben, und der Graf hatte beschlossen, ihr ein würdiges Denkmal zu errichten. Der Architekt Johann Henrici sowie der Bildhauer Johann Martin Fischer waren mit der Anfertigung einer aufwendigen Grabstätte beauftragt worden, in der die Gräfin am 27. März zur letzten Ruhe gebettet wurde;[2] zur selben Zeit befasste sich Wallsegg mit dem Vorhaben, ein Requiem in Auftrag zu geben, das jeweils zum Jahrestag des Todes seiner Gattin aufgeführt werden sollte. Dass die Wahl des Grafen auf Mozart fiel, mag auf den Ratschlag gemeinsamer Bekannter erfolgt sein.[3] Obwohl Mozart in Wien keinen besonderen Ruf als Komponist sakraler Musik genoss, ist bei ihm doch ein wachsendes Interesse an dieser Gattung seit den 1780er Jahren festzustellen.

Der Graf war ein begeisterter Amateurmusiker, und aus den überlieferten Beständen seines Musikarchivs geht hervor, dass er von den Wiener Musikalienhändlern die jeweils neuesten Kompositionen bezog, einschließlich der Werke Mozarts aus den 1780er und 1790er Jahren.[4] Wallsegg hatte mitunter die Angewohnheit, Werke direkt und anonym bei den Komponisten in Auftrag zu geben und sich von ihnen die Eigentümerschaft exklusiv zu sichern; die Musiker des Grafen ließen sich darauf ein, ihn als den Verfasser der jeweiligen Stücke anzusehen.[5] So verfuhr Wallsegg auch mit Mozart, indem ein Abgesandter seines Wiener Anwalts Johann Nepomuk Sortschan spätestens im August 1791 dem Komponisten ein entsprechendes Anliegen per Brief übermittelte.[6] Mozart forderte die Summe von 50 Dukaten (225 Florin), die Hälfte des für gewöhnlich für eine Oper anfallenden Entgelts; 25 Dukaten waren wahrscheinlich sofort fällig.

Mozart begann die Arbeit am Requiem nicht vor Ende September oder Anfang Oktober, nachdem er von den ersten Vorstellungen von *La Clemenza di Tito* in Prag nach Wien zurückgekehrt war. Ende November erkrankte er und verstarb in den frühen Morgenstunden des 5. Dezember, das Requiem unvollendet zurücklassend. Es ist kaum anzunehmen, dass sich Mozart im letzten Stadium seiner Krankheit nicht der Ironie des Schicksals bewusst war, dass er, kränkelnd und möglicherweise dem Tod ins Auge sehend, ausgerechnet an einem Requiem arbeitete. Doch dies soll nicht für seine allgemeine psychische Verfassung während der Arbeit an der Totenmesse stehen, denn in diese Zeit fielen auch erfreuliche Ereignisse wie die erfolgreiche Uraufführung der *Zauberflöte*.[7]

Wie gewohnt, begann Mozart die Komposition des Requiems, indem er zuerst die Vokalpartien sowie das Continuo in der Partitur notierte und die meisten Notensysteme für die Instrumente leer ließ, in der Absicht, diese später zu füllen. Als er verstarb, lagen in dieser Form das *Kyrie*, von der Sequenz die Sätze *Dies irae* bis *Confutatis* sowie das Offertorium (*Domine Jesu* und *Hostias*) geschlossen vor. Der Introitus war als einziger Satz vollständig orchestriert, vom *Lacrimosa* konnte Mozart nur noch die ersten acht Takte als Chorsatz mit Continuostimme niederschreiben. Bald nach Mozarts Tod wurde die Instrumentation des *Kyrie* in der Partitur des Komponisten von zwei unbekannten Autoren fertiggestellt. Gewöhnlich wird Mozarts ehemaliger Schüler Franz Jakob Freystädtler für einen der Urheber gehalten, was jedoch unzutreffend ist; auch die Identifikation Süßmayrs als Urheber ist problematisch.[8] Der Grund für diese Zuschreibungen mag darin liegen, dass am 10. Dezember 1791 in St. Michael eine Totenmesse für Mozart abgehalten wurde und in dieser angeblich Teile des Requiems zur Aufführung kamen.[9]

Mozarts Frau Constanze begann schon bald mit der Suche nach einem geeigneten Komponisten, der das Werk vollenden sollte. Sie entschied sich für Joseph Eybler (1765–1846), der bereits bei einer Reihe von Projekten Mozarts mitgewirkt hatte, einschließlich der Proben für *Così fan tutte*; Mozart hatte ihm 1790 eine ausgezeichnete Referenz geschrieben. Eybler vereinbarte am 21. Dezember 1791 vertraglich mit Constanze, das Requiem „Mitte der kommenden Fastenzeit" (d. h. Mitte März 1792) fertig zu haben. Er konnte die fehlenden Streicherstimmen vom *Dies irae* an bis zum *Confutatis* vervollständigen, außerdem fanden einige Passagen für Holz- und Blechbläser direkten Eingang in Mozarts autographe Partitur. Eybler fügte dem unvollendeten *Lacrimosa* noch zwei Takte hinzu, bevor er seine Arbeit aufgab und Constanze die Partitur wieder aushändigte, wahrscheinlich weil er Anfang 1792 zum Musikdirektor an der Karmeliterkirche (St. Josef) ernannt worden war.

Daraufhin wandte sich Constanze an Franz Xaver Süßmayr (1766–1803). Süßmayr war 1788 nach Wien gezogen und könnte Mozart 1790 zum ersten Mal getroffen haben, als beide Komponisten Rezitative zu einem Pasticcio auf der Grundlage von Guglielmis *La quacquera spirituosa* (KV deest/SmWV 285) verfassten.[10] Es wird zwar allgemein angenommen, Süßmayr habe in Wien vor dem Requiem-Auftrag nur ein sakrales Werk geschrieben,[11] in Tat und Wahrheit hatte er während seiner Studienzeit in Kremsmünster (ca. 1784–88) viel Musik für die Kirche komponiert und durfte daher kaum mehr als unerfahren auf diesem Gebiet gelten.[12] Mozarts einzige nachweisbare Beziehung zu Süßmayr datiert aus der Mitte des Jahres 1791, als Süßmayr in seiner Eigenschaft als Kopist das Material für *Die Zauberflöte* vorbereitete. Obwohl in vielen Darstellungen aus den 1790er Jahren Süßmayr als Mozarts Schüler bezeichnet wird, sind keine musikalischen Dokumente oder andere Quellen aus Mozarts Zeit erhalten geblieben, welche diese Behauptung stützen könnten.[13] Die zahlreichen wenig schmeichelhaften und neckenden Bemerkungen über Süßmayr in Mozarts letzten Briefen legen eine Haltung nahe, die nicht gerade auf übertrieben hohen Respekt gegenüber einem getreuen Schreibgehilfen schließen lässt.

Nach der Übergabe der Requiem-Partitur durch Constanze sah sich Süßmayr vor die Entscheidung gestellt, entweder dort anzufangen, wo Eybler aufgehört hatte, oder eine ganz neue Partitur zu erstellen. Süßmayr entschied sich zu Letzterem, und da Introitus wie auch *Kyrie* bereits vollständig vorlagen, begann er, das Requiem vom *Dies irae* an neu abzuschreiben, wobei er die Handschriften Mozarts und Eyblers auseinanderhielt.[14] Zwar orientierte sich Süßmayr in seiner Instrumentierung in manchem an Eyblers Arbeit, doch ließ er im Verlauf seiner Vervollständigung mehr und mehr von dessen Notat ab. Da Eybler nach dem *Dies irae* keine Holz- und Blechbläser eingetragen und in *Domine Jesu* und *Hostias* überhaupt nichts notiert hatte, waren seine Vorarbeiten für die Vollendung des Requiems ohnehin von begrenztem Wert.

Zusätzlich zu der Aufgabe, eine vollständige Orchestrierung zu erstellen, hatte Süßmayr eine noch schwierigere Herausforderung zu bewältigen: das *Lacrimosa* zu vollenden, das nach dem achten Takt abbrach, sowie Sanctus, Benedictus, Agnus Dei und Lux aeterna völlig neu zu komponieren – jene Sätze, zu denen Mozart in seinem Partiturtorso überhaupt nichts vermerkt hatte. Während der vergangenen 200 Jahre wurden so fruchtlose wie endlose Debatten darüber geführt, ob Süßmayrs Arbeiten ausschließlich auf eigenen Ideen beruhten oder ob er auf vermutlich verloren gegangene Entwürfe Mozarts zurückgreifen konnte. Für die Existenz solcher Skizzen spricht laut den Befürwortern die hohe Qualität einiger Passagen, vor allem im *Agnus Dei*, die sich an die Kompositionsweise in den von Mozart entworfenen Sätzen anlehnt. Gemäß dieser Theorie lagen Stilmerkmale wie diese nicht innerhalb Süßmayrs Fähigkeiten. Jene, die nicht von hypothetischen Skizzen Mozarts ausgehen, teilen die geringe Wertschätzung gegenüber Süßmayr, ziehen allerdings die Güte der in Frage stehenden Abschnitte in Zweifel, mit dem Hinweis auf eine angeblich mangelhafte Inspiration und technische Inkompetenz; nicht selten werden gerade diese Stellen von den Befürwortern der Skizzentheorie besonders gelobt.

Süßmayr selbst hielt daran fest, Sanctus, Benedictus und Agnus Dei vollumfänglich als seine eigenen Schöpfungen zu bezeichnen. In diesem Sinne informierte er um 1794 offenbar den Mozart-Biographen Franz Niemetschek.[15] Süßmayrs umfangreichstes Zeugnis bezüglich seiner Rolle ist ein Brief, den er 1800 an seinen Verleger Breitkopf schrieb. Darin hält er fest: „Das Sanctus – Benedictus und Agnus Dei – ist ganz neu von mir verfertigt; nur hab ich mir erlaubt, um dem Werke mehr Einförmigkeit zu geben, die Fuge des Kyrie, bei dem Verse – cum Sanctis etc. zu wiederhohlen." Außerdem behauptet Süßmayr, er habe „noch bey Lebzeiten Mozarts die schon in Musik gesetzen Stücke öfters mit ihm durchgespielt, und gesungen" und dass sich Mozart „mit mir über die Ausarbeitung dieses Werkes sehr oft besprochen, und mir den Gang und die Gründe seiner Instrumentirung mitgetheilt hatte."[16] Dieser letzte Satz ist mit Vorsicht zu behandeln, da Süßmayr zu Übertreibungen neigte, was seine Beziehung zu Mozart anging: In einem Brief vom August 1797 gab er an, er habe unter Mozarts Anleitung eine Oper, *Der rauschige Hans* (SmWV 208), geschrieben. Tatsächlich aber datiert die Oper aus dem Jahr 1788, noch bevor ein erstes Treffen zwischen Mozart und Süßmayr anzunehmen ist.[17]

Mehr als 30 Jahre später erinnerte sich Mozarts Schwägerin Sophie Haibel daran, Süßmayr in der Nacht des 4. Dezember 1791 am Bett des Komponisten gesehen zu haben. Mozart habe damals erklärt, wie das Requiem zu vollenden sei. Der Wahrheitsgehalt der Aussage, Süßmayr und Mozart hätten im letzten Stadium von Mozarts Krankheit Teile des Requiems gesungen, muss, wie auch derjenige einer später noch von Constanze persönlich gemachten Bemerkung, in Frage gestellt werden.[18] Ähnlich schwach ist die Beweislage hinsichtlich der Existenz von Entwürfen Mozarts für den letzten Teil des Requiems. Diese Annahme geht auf die überlieferte Aussage zurück, derzufolge Constanze an Süßmayr einige Zettel mit Noten darauf gegeben haben soll, die sie auf Mozarts Pult gefunden hatte.[19] Einige Teile der autographen Partitur Süßmayrs lassen allerdings tiefgreifende Korrekturen erkennen, was die These abschwächt, er habe mit vorgegebenem Material gearbeitet; im *Osanna* wurde sogar das Fugenthema verändert.[20] Falls für diese Sätze wirklich Skizzen Mozarts existiert haben sollten, können diese nicht besonders ausführlich gewesen sein.

Ein einzelnes Skizzenblatt für das Requiem in Mozarts Handschrift ist tatsächlich überliefert, aber dessen Inhalt wurde von Süßmayr nicht verwendet und war ihm wahrscheinlich auch gar nicht bekannt.[21] Neben einem Entwurf zur Ouvertüre der *Zauberflöte* enthält das Blatt eine ausgearbeitete Fassung der kanonischen Passagen der Takte 7–11 des *Rex tremendae* und eine sonst nicht weiter bekannte Skizze einer *Amen*-Fuge, unzweifelhaft als Schluss der Sequenz konzipiert. Mozart hatte in der *Amen*-Skizze augenscheinlich Schwierigkeiten mit der dichtgedrängten Anordnung der Stimmen, und es ist unklar, ob der Komponist ernsthaft daran dachte, sie in der vorliegenden Form in das Requiem zu integrieren. Eine Transkription der Skizze ist im Anhang der Partiturausgabe mitgeteilt.

Nachdem Süßmayr seine Partitur des Requiems vom *Dies irae* bis zum *Agnus Dei* beendet hatte, fügte er dem Werk zur zyklischen Abrundung noch einen Teil von Mozarts Introitus sowie das *Kyrie* (beides mit neuer Textunterlegung) als Abschluss hinzu. Überdies ergänzte er einige Generalbassbezifferungen im *Kyrie* und versah die Anfangsseite schließlich mit einer – wenig überzeugenden – Imitation von Mozarts Unterschrift und der Jahresangabe 1792. Danach händigte Süßmayr das vervollständigte Manuskript, allgemein als *Ablieferungspartitur* bezeichnet, Constanze aus. Bevor sie die Partitur an Wallsegg weiterreichte, ließ Constanze mindestens eine Abschrift für sich selbst erstellen, gegen die ursprünglich vereinbarte Exklusivität zwischen Mozart und dem Grafen handelnd.

Die Uraufführung des Requiems fand am 2. Januar 1793 statt, als Benefizkonzert für Constanze und ihre Kinder, und wurde von Baron van Swieten veranstaltet. Die Partitur wurde von der Witwe zur Verfügung gestellt, die auch für ein Konzert am 20. April 1796 in Leipzig ihr persönliches Exemplar bereitstellte. Diese Aufführungen wie auch die an den preußischen König sowie an den sächsischen Kurfürsten gesandten Abschriften sorgten bereits vor Drucklegung für eine unerwartet rasche Verbreitung des Requiems. Weitere Aufführungen fanden 1796 im Stift Kremsmünster, wahrscheinlich unter Süßmayrs Mitwirkung, und 1798 in Graz statt. Wallsegg selbst ließ das Requiem zum ersten Mal am 14. Dezember 1793 in der Abtei in der Wiener Neustadt aufführen; es folgte ein weiteres Konzert am 14. Februar 1794, dem dritten Jahrestag des Todes der Gräfin, in der Kirche Maria Schutz auf dem Semmering. Ob Wallsegg bis zu seinem Tod 1827 das Werk nochmals zur Aufführung brachte, ist nicht bekannt.

Der Erstdruck des Requiems erschien in der ersten Hälfte des Jahres 1800 bei Breitkopf & Härtel in Leipzig im Druck; unter anderem wurde dafür das Werkmanuskript aus Constanzes persönlichem Besitz verwendet. Mehr als 100 Exemplare des Originaldrucks haben bis heute überdauert – ein Beweis für die traurige Berühmtheit, die das Requiem seit seinen Anfängen umgibt.

Hauptquelle für die Neuedition einschließlich des vorliegenden Klavierauszugs ist die *Ablieferungspartitur*, die von Süßmayr zusammengestellt und von Constanze Mozart an den Grafen Wallsegg übergeben worden war. Mozarts Partiturentwurf von Sequenz und Offertorium diente als Vergleichsquelle, wobei Eyblers nachträgliche Zusätze unberücksichtigt blieben. Beide Manuskripte gehören heute zu den Beständen der Österreichischen Nationalbibliothek. Weiteres zu den Quellen und Editionsprinzipien findet sich im Revisionsbericht der Partiturausgabe (EP 11035).

Die Klavierreduktion fußt auf dem älteren Auszug von Friedrich Ferdinand Brissler, wurde jedoch vom Verlag neu durchgesehen und teilweise revidiert. Zur spieltechnischen Erleichterung sind Haken für die Verteilung der Noten zwischen beiden Händen eingefügt worden. Ferner wurde die Angabe der beteiligten Orchesterinstrumente präzisiert. Alle Studierbuchstaben sind praxisbezogen neu gesetzt.

Herzlich bedanken möchte ich mich bei den Mitarbeitern der Österreichischen Nationalbibliothek, des Stifts Kremsmünster und der Universitätsbibliothek Frankfurt am Main für die Bereitstellung von Dokumenten sowie bei Matthias Röder, Ingrid Schubert, Joshua Rifkin, Ian Allan, Michael Lorenz und Christoph Wolff für die vielen wertvollen Hinweise.

Cambridge, MA, im Juni 2009 *David Black*
(Übersetzung: Anja Bühnemann)

---

[1] Die wichtigste Quelle für die Entstehungsgeschichte des Requiems im Zusammenhang mit Wallsegg ist ein Bericht seines Dienstboten Anton Herzog. Die Darstellung war im 19. Jahrhundert bereits Otto Jahn und Ludwig von Köchel bekannt und wurde seither verschiedentlich „wiederentdeckt". Der Bericht wurde vollständig erstmals von Otto Erich Deutsch veröffentlicht: *Zur Geschichte von Mozarts Requiem*, in: ÖMZ 19 (1964), S. 49–60. Siehe auch Andrea Worliz-Wellspacher: *Der Bote des Requiembestellers*, in: *Wiener Geschichtsblätter* 45 (1990), S. 197–219, sowie Walther Brauneis: *,Dies irae, Dies illa – Tag des Zorns, Tag der Klage'. Auftrag, Entstehung und Vollendung von Mozarts ‚Requiem'*, in: *Jahrbuch des Vereins für Geschichte der Stadt Wien* 47/48 (1991/92), S. 33–50.

[2] Das Grab auf der Stuppacher Au, zwischen Wallseggs Schloss und dem Dorf Gloggnitz gelegen, wurde während der Napoleonischen Kriege zerstört und ist nicht mehr vorhanden. Als Todesursache wurde „hitziges Faulfieber" angegeben; es gibt bislang keinen Anlass zur Vermutung, die Gräfin sei im Kindbett gestorben.

[3] Wallsegg besaß in Wien ein Haus, in dem eine Etage von Michael Puchberg gemietet war, der Mozart ab 1788 namhafte Geldsummen lieh; im Dezember 1791 verkaufte Wallsegg das Haus an Franz Wilhelm von Natorp, einen weiteren Bekannten Mozarts.

[4] Siehe Worliz-Wellspacher: *Der Bote des Requiembestellers* und Walther Brauneis: *Franz Graf Wallsegg – Mozarts Auftraggeber für das Requiem: Neue Forschungsergebnisse zur Musikpflege auf Schloß Stuppach*, in: *Musik Mitteleuropas in der 2. Hälfte des 18. Jahrhunderts*, hrsg. von Pavol Polák, Bratislava 1993, S. 207–221.

[5] Siehe Otto Biba: *Par Monsieur François Comte de Wallsegg*, in: *Mitteilungen der Internationalen Stiftung Mozarteum* 29, Nr. 3/4 (1981), S. 34–50.

[6] Dieser Brief ging verloren, wie auch alle übrigen Briefe Wallseggs an Mozart; doch Constanze und Mozarts früher Biograph Niemetschek beziehen sich auf sie. Siehe Christoph Wolff: *Mozarts Requiem: Geschichte · Musik · Dokumente · Partitur des Fragments*, Kassel 1991, S. 122 ff. und 138 ff. Die Mär von dem „grauen Boten" ist eine Erfindung des Dichters Franz Grillparzer aus dem 19. Jahrhundert.

[7] Die Behauptung, am 4. Dezember 1791 habe eine Probe des Requiems mit einigen Darstellern der *Zauberflöte* „am Totenbett" stattgefunden, rührt von einem 35 Jahre nach diesem angeblichen Ereignis geschriebenen und anonym verfassten Nachruf her. Da einige der hierin kolportierten Fakten falsch sind, ist es zweifelhaft, ob eine solche Probe je stattgefunden hat.

[8] Michael Lorenz: *Freystädtler's supposed copying in the autograph of K. 626: A case of mistaken identity*. Beitrag zum Kongress *Mozart's Choral Music: Composition, Contexts, Performance*, Bloomington, 12. Februar 2006.

[9] Eine Dokumentation dieses Gottesdienstes erstellte als erster Walther Brauneis: *Unveröffentlichte Nachrichten zum Dezember 1791 aus einer Wiener Lokalzeitung*, in: *Mitteilungen der Internationalen Stiftung Mozarteum* 39 (1991), S. 165–168.

[10] Zu Mozarts Rezitativ siehe Dexter Edge: *Attributing Mozart (I): Three Accompanied Recitatives*, in: *Cambridge Opera Journal* 13 (2001), S. 197–237.

[11] Ein *Alleluia* für Bass und Orchester (SmWV 127), wahrscheinlich für Francesco Benucci geschrieben, der die Titelpartie in Mozarts *Le nozze di Figaro* sang sowie den Leporello in der Wiener Aufführung des *Don Giovanni* und den Guglielmo in *Così fan tutte*.

[12] Zu Süßmayrs Biographie siehe Henry Hausner: *Franz Xaver Süßmayr*, Wien, 1964; Rosemary Hilmar: *Das Bierhaus „Zum grünen Baum", die gefährliche Gesellschaft und Franz Xaver Süßmayr als Zeuge vor Gericht im Spiegel seiner Zeit*, in: *Wiener Figaro* 54, Nr. 3/4 (1997): S. 3–22; Johann Winterberger: *Franz Xaver Süssmayr: Leben, Umwelt und Gestalt*, Frankfurt/M. 1999.

[13] Es ist möglich, dass Süßmayr einer der „2 Scholaren" war, auf die sich Mozart in einem Brief vom Mai 1790 bezog; siehe Wilhelm A. Bauer, Otto Erich Deutsch et al.: *Mozart: Briefe und Aufzeichnungen*, Bd. 4, Kassel, 2005, S. 108.

[14] Denkbar wäre auch, dass Süßmayr von Constanze eine heute verschollene Kopie der autographen Partitur erhielt und die Unterscheidung der Handschriften vom Kopisten bereits vorweggenommen worden war.

[15] Niemetschek schrieb 1810 an seinen Verleger Kühnel, das Requiem sei „von Süßmeyer vollendet u.[nd] z.[war] vom Sanktus angefangen. Und dieß hat Süßmeyer mir selbst gesagt, da er vor 17 Jahren bey mir wohnte und die Oper ,Il Musselmanno in Napoli' [*Il turco in Italia* SmWV 211] für Bondinis Theater bey mir vollendete." (*Briefe*, Bd. VI, S. 725).

[16] Wolff: *Mozarts Requiem*, S. 145. Einem Bericht Constanzes zufolge, der nur aus zweiter Hand überliefert und beinahe vier Jahrzehnte später entstanden ist, beruht die Wiederverwendung des *Kyrie* für das „Cum sanctis" auf einer Anregung Mozarts; Richard Maunder: *Mozart's Requiem: On preparing a new edition*, Oxford, 1988, S. 17.

[17] Süßmayr bezeichnete das Werk als „ein Operett, genannt der rauschige Hans von dem seeligen Hrn. P. Maurus Lindemayr, wozu ich hier [Wien] unter der Leitung des seeligen, unsterblichen Mozarts die Musik setzte"; Hausner: *Franz Xaver Süßmayr*, S. 40.

[18] Wolff: *Mozarts Requiem*, S. 125. Drei Wochen vor Mozarts Tod war Süßmayr zum Aushilfsmusiker am Burgtheater berufen worden. Gemäß der Besoldungsliste des Theaters bezog er ein Gehalt von 25 fl für seine Dienste während der Woche um den 3. Dezember 1791 (Österreichische Nationalbibliothek Wien, Theatersammlung, M 4000). Süßmayr wäre demzufolge in der Nacht des 4. Dezembers eher bei einer Aufführung von Paisiellos *La Molinara* anzutreffen gewesen als an Mozarts Bett.

[19] Zitiert in Wolff: *Mozarts Requiem*, S. 152, und Karl Wagner (Hrsg.): *Abbé Maximilian Stadler: seine Materialien zur Geschichte der Musik unter den österreichischen Regenten*, Kassel 1974, S. 142.

[20] Siehe Richard Maunder: *Süßmayr's work in Mozart's Requiem: a study of the autograph score*, in: *Mozart-Studien* 7 (1997), S. 57–80.

[21] Staatsbibliothek zu Berlin, Mus. ms. autogr. W. A. Mozart zu: 620, Anh. 102 = 620a, 626 (Skb 1791a; vgl. Ulrich Konrad: *Mozart-Werkverzeichnis. Kompositionen · Fragmente · Skizzen · Bearbeitungen · Abschriften · Texte*, Kassel 2005).

Preface

The Requiem K. 626, Mozart's only setting of the *missa pro defunctis*, was commissioned by Count Franz von Wallsegg (1763–1827).[1] Wallsegg's wife, Anna (née Prenner von Flammberg) had died on 14 February 1791 at the age of 20, and the Count determined to create an appropriate memorial for her. The architect Johann Henrici and the sculptor Johann Martin Fischer were brought in to design an elaborate tomb, in which the Countess was interred on March 27;[2] at the same time, Wallsegg had the idea of commissioning a musical setting of the requiem mass, to be performed on anniversaries of her death. The Count's choice of Mozart may have occurred through the urging of mutual acquaintances; although Mozart had not maintained a high profile as a composer of church music in Vienna, he had shown an increasing interest in the form since the late 1780s.[3]

The Count was an enthusiastic amateur musician, and surviving portions of his music archive show that he obtained the latest music from Viennese music dealers, including works by Mozart, throughout the 1780s and 90s.[4] Wallsegg was occasionally in the habit of anonymously procuring works directly from their composers, for which he retained the sole ownership; the Count's musicians would humour him that he himself was the author.[5] This procedure was followed with Mozart, when a representative of Wallsegg's Viennese lawyer Johann Nepomuk Sortschan delivered the commission in a letter to the composer by August at the latest.[6] Mozart requested a fee of 50 ducats (225 florins), half of the usual fee for an opera; 25 ducats may have been paid in advance.

Mozart did not begin work on the Requiem until late September or October, when he returned to Vienna after the first productions of *La Clemenza di Tito* in Prague. He fell ill towards the end of November, and died in the early morning of 5 December, the Requiem still unfinished. In the late stages of his illness, it is difficult to believe that Mozart did not reflect on the irony of writing a Requiem while facing lengthy incapacitation and possibly death. However, this should not be taken as his general state of mind while writing the mass, a time punctuated by several happy events including the successful first run of *Die Zauberflöte*.[7]

Following his usual procedure, Mozart began the composition of the Requiem by writing the vocal parts and continuo into the score in full, leaving most of the instrumental staves blank with the expectation of filling them in later. By his death, Mozart had completed the Introit and *Kyrie*, all but the last movement of the Sequence (*Dies irae* through *Confutatis*), and the Offertorium (*Domine Jesu-Hostias*) in this form. In addition, he had completely orchestrated the Introit, and written the first eight bars only of the *Lacrimosa* in its vocal-continuo form. Soon after Mozart's death, the instrumentation of the *Kyrie* was completed in the composer's score by two unknown hands; the usual identification of one as Mozart's former student Franz Jakob Freystädtler is incorrect, and the identification of the other as Süssmayr is problematic.[8] The reason for this activity may have been a requiem mass for Mozart that took place at the church of St. Michael on 10 December 1791, at which some form of the Requiem was allegedly performed.[9]

Mozart's wife Constanze soon began searching for a suitable composer to complete the work. She settled on Joseph Eybler (1765–1846), who had been involved with a number of musical projects by Mozart including the rehearsals for *Così fan tutte*; Mozart had written a glowing testimonial for him in 1790. Eybler contracted with Constanze on 21 December 1791 to complete the Requiem 'by the middle of the coming Lent', i.e. mid-March 1792. He was able to complete the missing string parts for the *Dies irae* through *Confutatis*, in addition to a number of passages for the woodwind and brass, entered directly into Mozart's autograph score. Eybler also added two bars to Mozart's unfinished *Lacrimosa* before abandoning the completion and handing the score back to Constanze, perhaps due to his appointment as director of music at the Karmeliterkirche (St. Josef) in early 1792.

Constanze next turned to Franz Xaver Süssmayr (1766–1803). Süssmayr had moved to Vienna in 1788, and may have met Mozart for the first time in 1790, when they both contributed recitatives to a pasticcio opera based on Guglielmi's *La quacquera spirituosa* (K. deest/SmWV 285).[10] Although he is known to have written only one sacred piece in Vienna prior to the Requiem commission,[11] Süssmayr had composed extensively for the church during his later student years at Kremsmünster (c. 1784–88) and could hardly be described as an inexperienced practitioner in this form.[12] Mozart's only known references to Süssmayr date from mid-1791, when Süssmayr was engaged as a copyist preparing material for *Die Zauberflöte*. Although many reports from the 1790s describe Süssmayr as Mozart's pupil, no surviving musical or documentary sources from Mozart's lifetime support this claim.[13] The many uncomplimentary and teasing references to Süssmayr in Mozart's late letters suggest his attitude was primarily one of detached bemusement rather than respect for a trusted amanuensis.

Upon delivery of the Requiem score from Constanze, Süssmayr was faced with a decision: whether to continue the completion from where Eybler had left off, or prepare a new score. Süssmayr opted for the latter, and, since the Introit and *Kyrie* were already complete, he began copying out the Requiem anew from the *Dies irae* onwards, distinguishing between Mozart's and Eybler's hands and omitting the work of the latter as he proceeded.[14] Süssmayr's subsequent orchestration often owes something to Eybler's work, but as Eybler had not entered woodwind and brass parts after the *Dies irae*, and had written nothing for the *Domine Jesu* and *Hostias*, his work was of only limited use in preparing the new completion.

In addition to the necessary task of filling in the orchestration, Süssmayr faced a more daunting challenge: finishing Mozart's *Lacrimosa*, which broke off after its eighth bar, and providing entirely new settings of the Sanctus, Benedictus, Agnus Dei and Lux aeterna, movements for which Mozart had provided absolutely nothing in his unfinished score. For the past two hundred years it has been matter of unresolvable and interminable debate whether the movements produced by Süssmayr were created solely from his own imagination or made use of hypothetical lost sketches by Mozart. Those for the existence of Mozart sketches have typically argued for the high quality of certain passages, particularly in the *Agnus Dei*, and observed instances of motivic integration supposedly consistent with the design of those movements outlined by Mozart. According to this theory, features such as these were beyond the capabilities of Süssmayr. Those against hypothetical Mozart sketches share a low opinion of Süssmayr, but disagree on the merits of the disputed movements, pointing to their alleged limited inspiration and technical incompetence, often the very same passages singled out by sketch proponents for particular praise.

Süssmayr himself was consistent in describing the *Sanctus*, *Benedictus* and *Agnus Dei* as entirely his own work. He may have informed Mozart's biographer Franz Niemetschek of this fact as early as 1794.[15] Süssmayr's most extended testimony concerning his role is a letter written to the publisher Breitkopf in 1800, in which he stated that "the Sanctus, Benedictus and Agnus Dei were wholly composed by me; but, in order to give the work greater uniformity, I took the liberty of repeating the *Kyrie* fugue at the line 'cum sanctis etc.'" In addition, Süssmayr claimed that Mozart had "frequently sung and played through with him the movements that were already composed ... frequently talked to me about the detailed working of this composition, and explained to me the know and the wherefore of his instrumentation."[16] This last sentence must be treated with caution, as Süssmayr was not averse to exaggerating his relationship with Mozart: in a letter of August 1797 he claimed that he had written an opera, *Der rauschige Hans* (SmWV 208) under the supervision of Mozart. In fact, the autograph of the opera is dated 1788, before Mozart and Süssmayr had probably met.[17]

More than thirty years after the event, Mozart's sister-in-law Sophie Haibel recalled seeing Süssmayr at the composer's bedside on the night of 4 December 1791, with Mozart explaining how the Requiem should be completed. The veracity of this report, as for an even later one by Constanze of herself, Süssmayr and Mozart singing through parts of the Requiem during Mozart's last illness must remain in question.[18] Likewise, the documentary evidence for the existence of Mozart sketches for the later part of the Requiem is weak, consisting of two similarly worded hearsay statements that Constanze gave Süssmayr some scraps of paper with music on them that she had found on Mozart's desk.[19] Some parts of Süssmayr's autograph score bear heavy corrections, weakening the case for him working from pre-existing material; in the *Osanna*, even the fugue subject itself was subject to change.[20] If Mozart sketches for these movements did indeed exist, they cannot have been very extensive.

A single sketch-leaf in Mozart's hand does in fact survive for the Requiem, but its contents were not used by Süssmayr and were probably unknown to him.[21] In addition to a sketch for the overture to *Die Zauberflöte*, the leaf contains a working-out of the canonic writing for the voices in b. 7–11 of the *Rex tremendae* and an otherwise unknown sketch for an *Amen* fugue, undoubtedly intended to close the Sequence. Mozart evidently had difficulty with the closely-spaced disposition of the voices in the *Amen* sketch, and it is unclear whether the composer seriously envisaged including it in the Requiem in its present form. A transcription is provided in the Appendix to this edition.

Having finished his score of the Requiem from the *Dies irae* to the end of the piece, Süssmayr attached Mozart's pre-existing score of the Introit and *Kyrie* in order to create the complete work. In addition, he added some missing figuring to the continuo part in the *Kyrie*, and inscribed a rather unconvincing imitation of Mozart's signature and the date 1792 on the opening page. Süssmayr then gave the completed manuscript, generally known as the *Ablieferungspartitur* ('delivery score') to Constanze. Before handing over this score to Wallsegg, Constanze had at least one copy made for herself, breaking the spirit and possibly the letter of the exclusive agreement between Mozart and the Count.

The first performance of the Requiem took place on 2 January 1793 at a benefit concert for Constanze and her children organised by Baron van Swieten. The score was provided by the widow, who furnished her personal copy again for a performance in Leipzig on 20 April 1796. These performances, as well as copies sent to the King of Prussia and the Elector of Saxony allowed the Requiem to get 'into the wild' well before its publication. Further performances occurred at Stift Kremsmünster in 1796, possibly with the involvement of Süssmayr, and Graz in 1798. Wallsegg's first performance of the Requiem occurred on 14 December 1793 at the Abbey Church in Wiener Neustadt, and was followed by a further performance on 14 February 1794, the anniversary of the Countess' death, at the church of Maria Schutz on Semmering. Wallsegg is not known to have made further use of the work before his death in 1827.

The Requiem was first published by the Leipzig house of Breitkopf & Härtel in the first half of 1800, using *inter alia* Constanze's personal exemplar of the work. More than 100 copies of the original print survive today, a testament to the notoriety surrounding the Requiem from its inception.

The principal source for our edition, including the present vocal score, is the *Ablieferungspartitur* of the Requiem, which was assembled by Süssmayr and delivered to Count Wallsegg by Constanze Mozart. Mozart's draft score of the Sequence and Offertory has served as a comparison source, although Eybler's subsequent additions to it are disregarded for the purposes of this edition. In a number of instances, Süssmayr seems to have changed Mozart's musical text intentionally. Very few of these changes can be regarded as superior to the original, but they have generally been retained, since reverting to Mozart's readings would require extensive editorial intervention in the surrounding parts. Both the *Ablieferungspartitur* and Mozart's draft score are preserved today at the Österreichische Nationalbibliothek in Vienna. For more information on the sources and the editorial procedures of this edition, see the Critical Report to the full score edition (EP 11035).

The piano reduction, based on the former Peters vocal score by Friedrich Ferdinand Brissler, was revised and optimised in many details. For practical purposes, signs for dividing the piano part between left and right hands have been added.

Furthermore, the participating orchestral instruments are indicated more precisely. In accordance with the full score edition, new study letters for rehearsal purposes have been incorporated.

I am grateful to the staff of the Österreichische Nationalbibliothek, Stift Kremsmünster and the Universitätsbibliothek Frankfurt am Main for the provision of materials, and to Matthias Röder, Ingrid Schubert, Joshua Rifkin, Ian Allan, Michael Lorenz and Christoph Wolff for many helpful comments.

Cambridge, MA, June 2009   *David Black*

---

[1] The most important source for the history of the Requiem from Wallsegg's perspective is an account by his servant Anton Herzog. It was already known to Otto Jahn and Ludwig von Köchel in the nineteenth century, but has been repeatedly 'discovered' since then. The report was first published in full in Otto Erich Deutsch, 'Zur Geschichte von Mozarts Requiem', *Österreichische Musikzeitschrift* 19 (1964): 49–60. See also Andrea Worliz-Wellspacher, 'Der Bote des Requiembestellers', *Wiener Geschichtsblätter* 45 (1990): 197–219 and Walther Brauneis, '"Dies irae, Dies illa – Tag des Zornes, Tag der Klage", Auftrag, Entstehung und Vollendung von Mozarts „Requiem"', *Jahrbuch des Vereins für Geschichte der Stadt Wien* 47–48 (1991–92): 33–50.

[2] The tomb, located on the Stuppacher Au between Wallsegg's palace and the village of Gloggnitz was damaged in the Napoleonic wars and is no longer extant. The cause of death was 'hitziges Faulfieber'; there is no evidence at present to support the suggestion that the Countess died in childbirth.

[3] Wallsegg owned a house in Vienna, one floor of which was rented by Michael Puchberg, who loaned Mozart substantial sums of money from 1788; in December 1791 Wallsegg sold the house to Franz Wilhelm von Natorp, another acquaintance of the composer.

[4] See Worliz-Wellspacher, 'Der Bote des Requiembestellers' and Walther Brauneis, 'Franz Graf Wallsegg – Mozarts Auftraggeber für das Requiem: Neue Forschungsergebnisse zur Musikpflege auf Schloß Stuppach', *Musik Mitteleuropas in der 2. Hälfte des 18. Jahrhunderts*, ed. Pavol Polák (Bratislava: 1993), 207–221.

[5] See Otto Biba, 'Par Monsieur François Comte de Wallsegg', *Mitteilungen der Internationalen Stiftung Mozarteum* 29, no. 3/4 (1981): 34–50.

[6] The letter (and further letters from Wallsegg to Mozart) are lost, but are referred to by Constanze and Mozart's early biographer Niemetschek; see Christoph Wolff, *Mozart's Requiem: Historical and Analytical Studies, Documents, Score* (Oxford: 1994), 126, 142. The story of the 'grey messenger' is a nineteenth-century invention by the poet Franz Grillparzer.

[7] The story that a 'death-bed rehearsal' of the Requiem took place on 4 December 1791 with a number of cast members from *Die Zauberflöte* derives from an anonymous obituary written more than 35 years after the alleged event. Many of the factual details in the obituary are incorrect and it is doubtful that such a rehearsal ever occurred.

[8] Michael Lorenz, 'Freystädtler's supposed copying in the autograph of K. 626: A case of mistaken identity', paper presented at the conference *Mozart's Choral Music: Composition, Contexts, Performance*, Bloomington, 12 February 2006.

[9] Documentation of this service was first reported in Walther Brauneis, 'Unveröffentliche Nachrichten zum Dezember 1791 aus einer Wiener Lokalzeitung', *Mitteilungen der Internationalen Stiftung Mozarteum* 39 (1991): 165–68.

[10] On Mozart's recitative, see Dexter Edge, 'Attributing Mozart (I): Three Accompanied Recitatives', *Cambridge Opera Journal* 13 (2001): 197–237.

[11] An *Alleluia* for bass and orchestra (SmWV 127), apparently intended for Francesco Benucci, who created the roles of Figaro in Mozart's *Le nozze di Figaro*, Leporello in the Viennese *Don Giovanni*, and Guglielmo in *Così fan tutte*.

[12] On Süssmayr's biography, see Henry Hausner, *Franz Xaver Süßmayr* (Vienna: Bergland Verlag, 1964); Rosemary Hilmar, 'Das Bierhaus „Zum grünen Baum", die gefährliche Gesellschaft und Franz Xaver Süßmayr als Zeuge vor Gericht im Spiegel seiner Zeit', *Wiener Figaro* 54, nos. 3/4 (1997): 3–22; Johann Winterberger, *Franz Xaver Süßmayr: Leben, Umwelt und Gestalt* (Frankfurt: 1999).

[13] It is possible that Süssmayr was one of the '2 Scholaren' to whom Mozart referred in a letter of May 1790; see Wilhelm A. Bauer, Otto Erich Deutsch et al., *Mozart: Briefe und Aufzeichnungen* (Kassel: 2005), IV.108.

[14] Alternatively, it is possible that Süssmayr received a now-lost copy of the autograph from Constanze, and the work of distinguishing the hands of Mozart and Eybler was achieved by the copyist.

[15] In 1810, Nietmetschek wrote to the publisher Kühnel that 'ist es [das Requiem] von Süßmeyer vollendet u. z. vom Sanktus angefangen. Und dieß hat Süßmeyer mir selbst gesagt, da er vor 17 Jahren bey mir wohnte und die Oper „Il Musselmanno in Neapoli" [*Il turco in Italia* SmWV 211] für Bondinis Theater bey mir vollendete'; *Briefe*, VI.725.

[16] Wolff, *Mozart's Requiem*, 146. According to a second-hand report of Constanze almost four decades after the event, the reuse of the *Kyrie* for the *Cum sanctis* was according to Mozart's suggestion; Richard Maunder, *Mozart's Requiem: On preparing a new edition* (Oxford: 1988), 17.

[17] Süssmayr described the work as 'ein Operett, genannt *der rauschige Hans von dem seeligen Hrn. P. Maurus Lindemayr*, wozu ich hier [Wien] unter der Leitung des seeligen, unsterblichen Mozarts die Musik setzte'; Hausner, *Franz Xaver Süßmayr*, 40.

[18] Wolff, *Mozart's Requiem*, 126, 170. Three weeks before Mozart's death, Süssmayr had been appointed temporary accompanist at the Burgtheater. According to the theatre's ledger, he received a payment of 25 fl for his duties there in the week of 3 December 1791 (Österreichische Nationalbibliothek Wien, Theatersammlung, M 4000). Süssmayr thus may have been at a performance of Paisiello's *La Molinara* on the night of 4 December, not at Mozart's bedside.

[19] Quoted in Wolff, *Mozart's Requiem*, 152, and Karl Wagner (ed.), *Abbé Maximilian Stadler: seine 'Materialien zur Geschichte der Musik unter den österreichischen Regenten'* (Kassel: 1974), 142.

[20] See Richard Maunder, 'Süßmayr's work in Mozart's Requiem: a study of the autograph score', *Mozart-Studien* 7 (1997): 57–80.

[21] Staatsbibliothek zu Berlin, Mus. ms. autogr. W. A. Mozart zu: 620, Anh. 102 = 620a, 626 (Skb 1791a; see Ulrich Konrad, *Mozart-Werkverzeichnis: Kompositionen · Fragmente · Skizzen · Bearbeitungen · Abschriften · Texte* [Kassel: 2005]).

BESETZUNG / ORCHESTRATION

Corno di Bassetto I / II

Fagotto I / II

Clarino I / II

Trombone I / II / III

Timpani

Violino I
Violino II
Viola
Violoncello
Contrabbasso

Organo

Soli:
Soprano, Alto, Tenore, Basso

Coro

REQUIEM

d-Moll · D minor
KV 626 / SmWV 105

Wolfgang Amadeus Mozart (1756–1791)
Ergänzung von Franz Xaver Süßmayr (1766–1803)
Herausgegeben von David Black

Introitus

1. Requiem aeternam

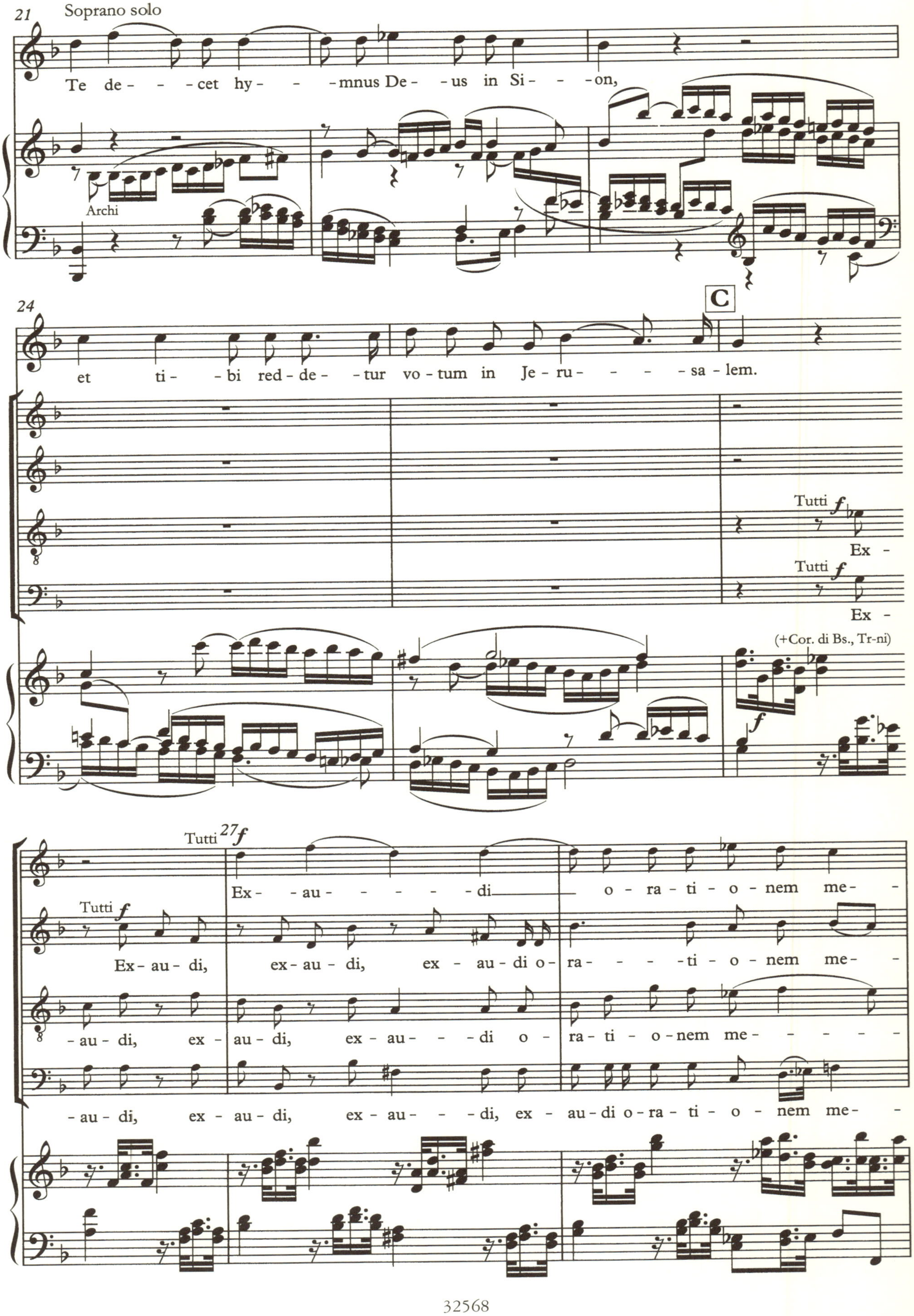
21
Soprano solo
Te de- - -cet hy- - - -mnus De- -us in Si- - -on,
Archi
24
C
et ti- -bi red-de- -tur vo-tum in Je-ru- - - - -sa-lem.
Tutti f
Ex-
Tutti f
Ex-
(+Cor. di Bs., Tr-ni)
Tutti 27 f
Ex- -au- - - - -di o-ra-ti-o-nem me-
Tutti f
Ex-au-di, ex-au-di, ex-au-di o-ra- - - -ti-o-nem me-
-au-di, ex-au-di, ex-au- - -di o-ra-ti-o-nem me- - - - -
-au-di, ex-au-di, ex-au- - - -di, ex-au-di o-ra-ti-o-nem me-

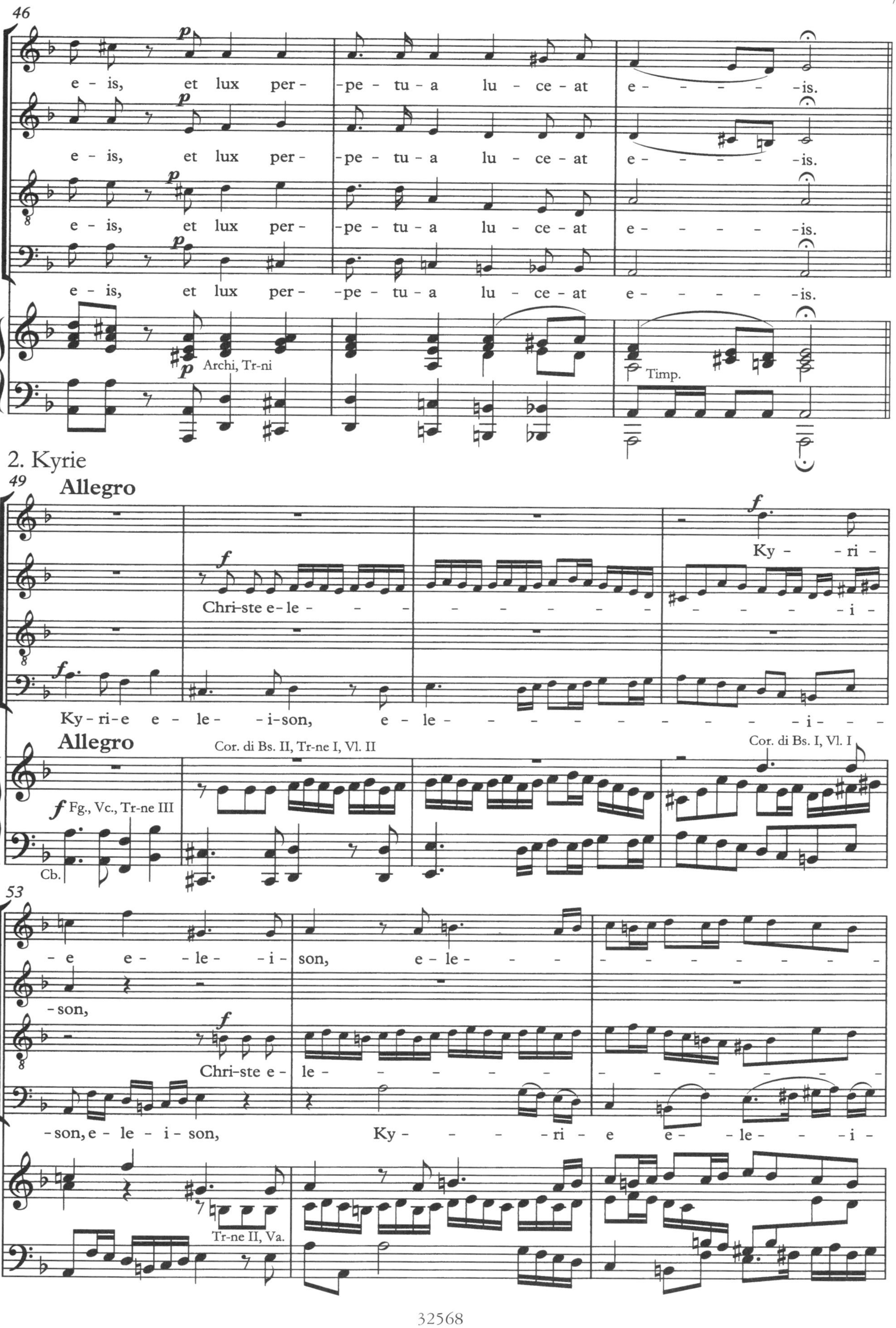
46
e - is, et lux per- -pe - tu - a lu - ce - at e - - - - -is.
Archi, Tr-ni
Timp.
2. Kyrie
49
Allegro
Ky - - ri -
Chri-ste e-le - - - - - - - - - - - - - - - i -
Ky-ri-e e - le - - i-son, e - le - - - - - - - - - - - - i - - -
Allegro
Cor. di Bs. II, Tr-ne I, Vl. II
Cor. di Bs. I, Vl. I
Fg., Vc., Tr-ne III
Cb.
53
-e e - -le- -i - son, e - le - - - - - - - - - - - -
-son,
Chri-ste e - le - - - - - - - - - - - - - -
-son, e - le - i - son, Ky - - - - -ri - e e- -le- - -i -
Tr-ne II, Va.

Sequenz

3. Dies irae

4. Tuba mirum

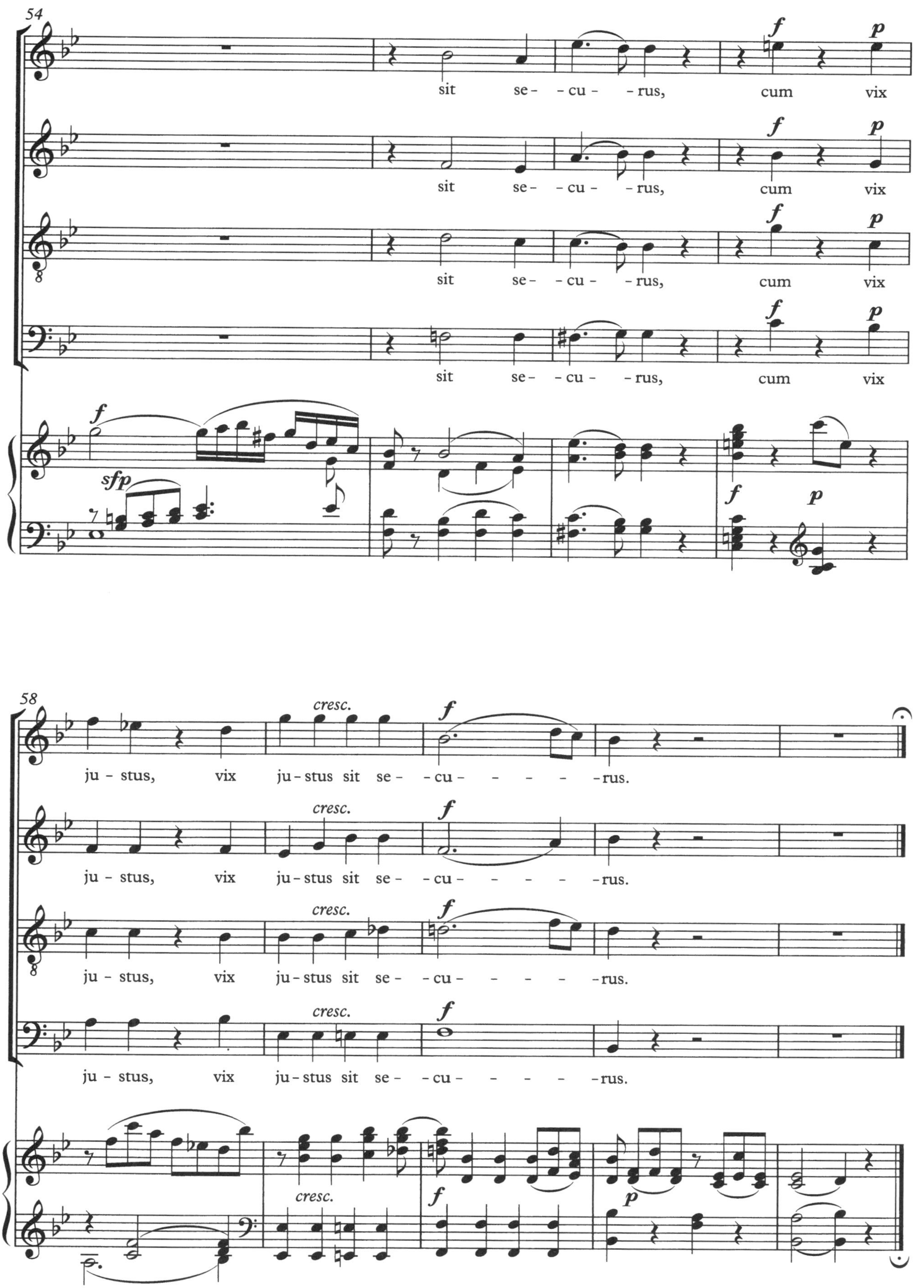
54
sit se - cu - rus, cum vix
f p
58
ju - stus, vix ju - stus sit se - cu - rus.
cresc.
f
sfp

5. Rex tremendae

6. Recordare

7. Confutatis

8. Lacrimosa

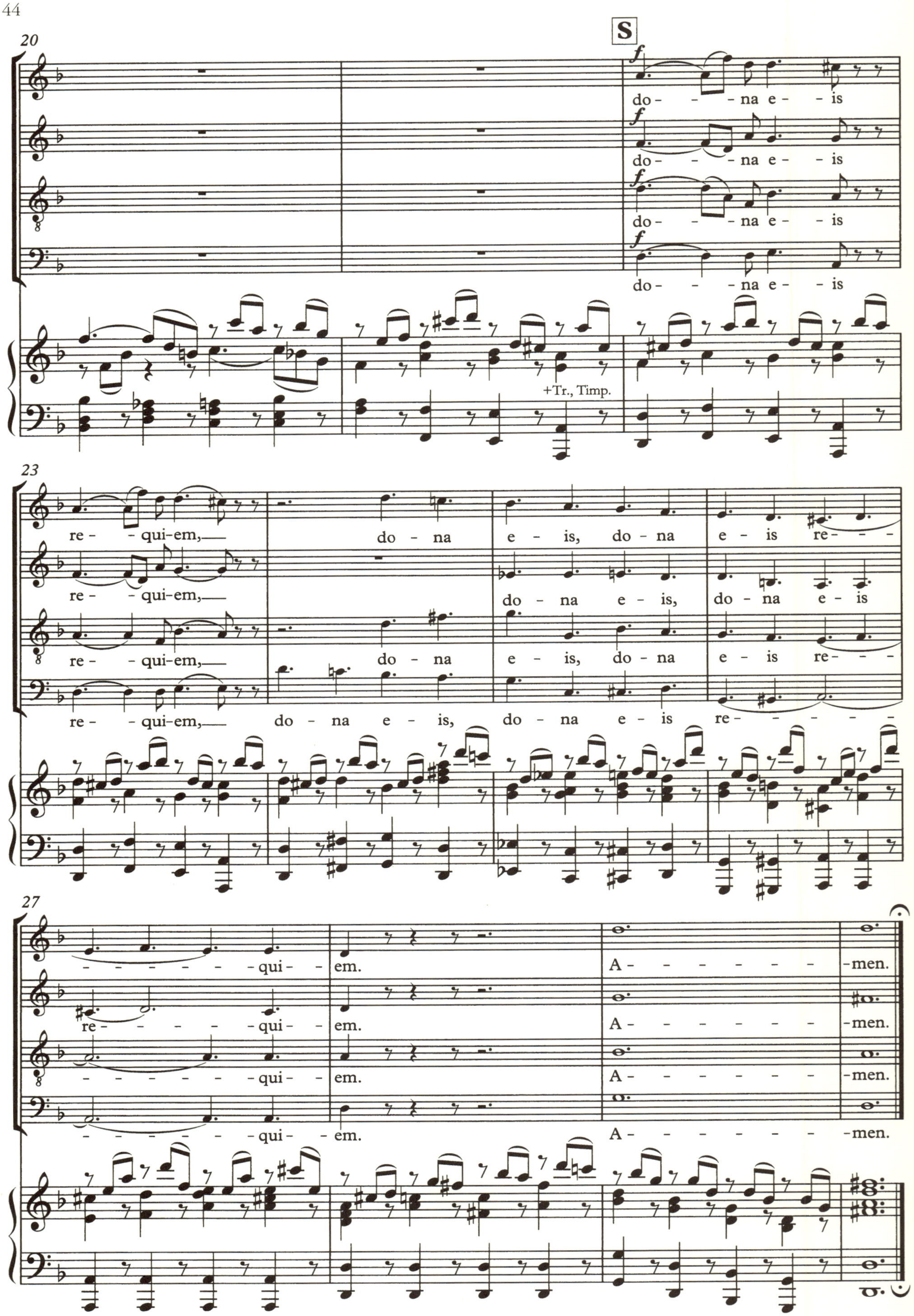
20
S
do- - na e- - is
+Tr., Timp.
23
re- - qui-em,
do - na e - is, do - na e - is re-
do - na e - is, do - na e - is
do - na e - is, do - na e - is re-
27
qui - em.
A - - - - - - - -men.

10. Hostias

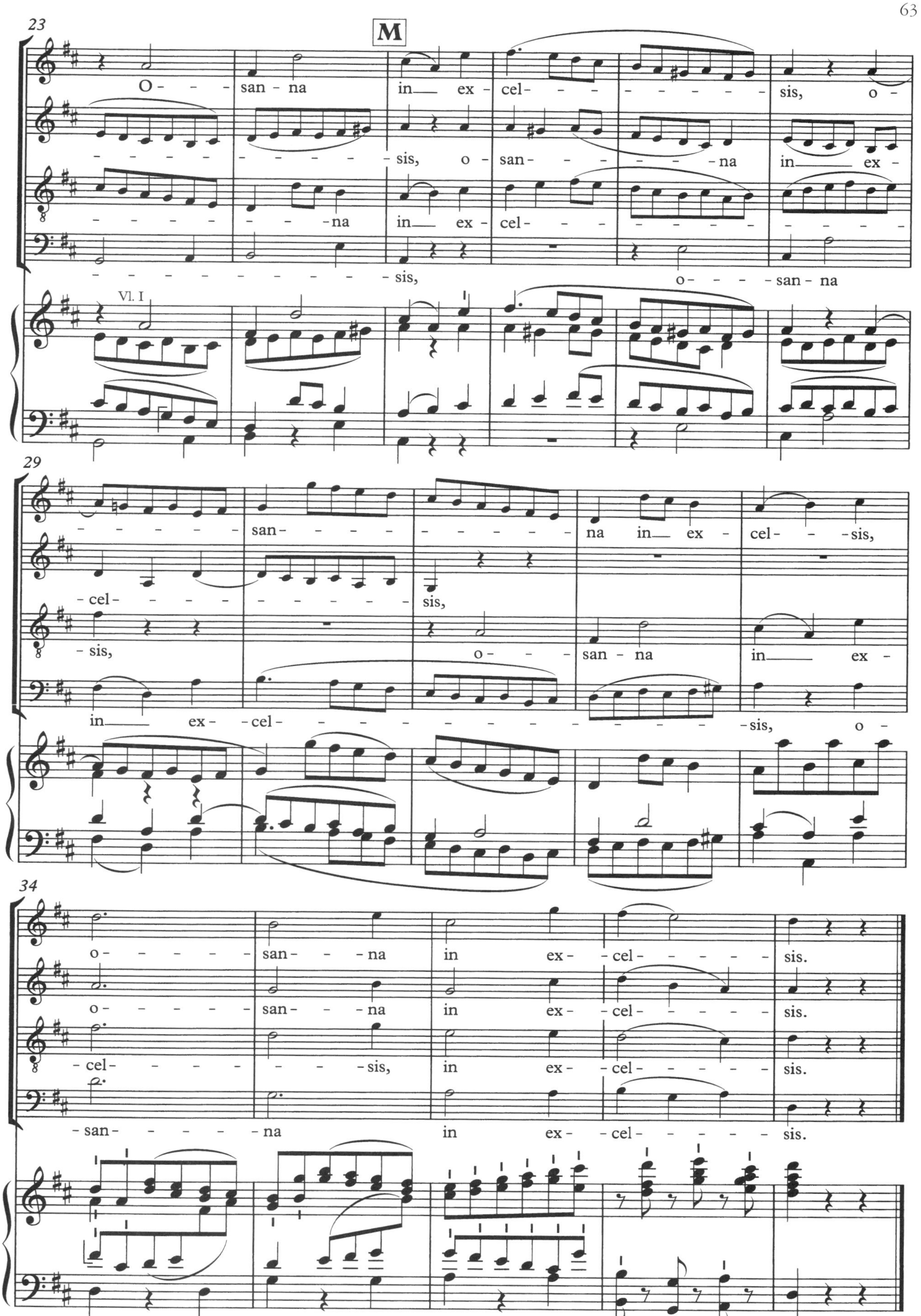
23
M
O- - - san- na in ex- cel- - - - - - - - - - sis, o-
- - - - - - - - - - - - - sis, o- san- - - - - - na in ex-
- - - - - - - - na in ex- cel- - - - - - - - - - - - - -
- - - - - - - - - - - - - sis, o- - - san- na
Vl. I
29
- - - - - - san- - - - - - - - - - - na in ex- cel- - sis,
- cel- - - - - - - - - - - - sis,
- sis, o- - - san- na in ex-
in ex- cel- - - - - - - - - - - - - - sis, o-
34
o- - - - - - san- - na in ex- cel- - - - - sis.
o- - - - - - san- - - na in ex- cel- - - - - sis.
- cel- - - - - - - - - sis, in ex- cel- - - - - - sis.
- san- - - - - - na in ex- cel- - - - - sis.

12. Benedictus

38
T
- ni, be-ne-di- - ctus qui ve- - nit, be-ne-
- ni, be-ne-di - ctus qui ve- - nit in no - mi-ne Do- - mi -
- ni, be-ne-di - ctus qui ve- - nit in no - mi-ne Do- - mi -
- ni, be-ne-di-ctus qui ve-nit in no - mi-ne
+Cor. di Bs., Fg.
fp
+Tr-ni
41
- di- - ctus qui ve- - nit in no- - - - - mi - ne Do- - mi-ni, be-ne-di-ctus
- ni, qui ve- - nit in no- - - - - mi - ne Do- - mi-ni, be-ne-
- ni, be-ne - di - ctus qui ve- - nit in no - - mi - ne Do- - mi-ni, be-ne-
Do-mi-ni, be-ne-di - ctus qui ve- - nit in no - - mi - ne Do- - mi-ni, be-ne-di-ctus
Archi, Fg.

Agnus Dei

13. Agnus Dei

Communio

14. Lux aeterna